Why
do people live on the
Streets?

Kaye Stearman

H O D D E R
Wayland

an imprint of Hodder Children's Books

© 2000 White-Thomson Publishing Ltd

Produced for Hodder Wayland by
White-Thomson Publishing Ltd
2/3 St Andrew's Place
Lewes
BN7 1UP

Other titles in this series:
Why do people drink alcohol?
Why do people take drugs?
Why do people gamble?
Why do people join gangs?
Why do people smoke?

Series concept: Alex Woolf
Editor: Liz Gogerly
Cover Design: Hodder Children's Books
Inside Design: Stonecastle Graphics Ltd

Published in Great Britain in 2000 by Hodder
Wayland, an imprint of Hodder Children's Books

A Catalogue record for this book is available from
the British Library.

ISBN 07502 27575

Printed and bound in Italy by G. Canale & C.S.p.A.,
Turin

Hodder Children's Books
A division of Hodder Headline Limited
338 Euston Road, London NW1 3BH

Picture acknowledgements
The publisher would like to thank the following
for their kind permission to use their pictures:

Associated Press 36, 43; Eye Ubiquitous/ J.Hulme 4/
David Cummings 8, 14/ Michael George 16/ Julia
Waterlow 20/ Jason Burke 24/ Johnstone 26/ Philip
Wolmuth 27/ Skjold 29; Format/ Lisa Woollett 38;
Sally and Richard Greenhill Picture Library 34;
Robert Harding/ Jeff Greenberg 42;
Hodder/Wayland Picture Library (title page),
(contents),10 (bottom), 24, 35, 37, 40, 44 (bottom)/
© Shelter 15/ Howard Davies 17/ Martyn Chillmaid
19/ J. Holmes 44 (top)/ Zak Waters 45; Impact/
Peter Arkell 4/ Adam Hinton 12; Panos/ Paul
Quayle 13/ Giacomo Pirozzi 25, 39; Popperfoto 10
(top), 11,15, 31, 32, 33; Rex Features/ Nina
Bermann 21; Chris Schwarz contents (top), 5, 9, 18,
22, 27, 28, 30, 33, 41 (top and bottom); Roger
Vlitos (cover), 7, 22

Contents

1. Life without a home

What is life like without a home?

Imagine your life without a proper home. You no longer have a bedroom for sleeping, a kitchen for cooking food or a bathroom for washing. Now imagine you have hardly any money. How would you manage?

You would need to find somewhere to sleep and keep your belongings. Maybe you could sleep in a empty building, on a park bench or in a bus shelter. If you are lucky you might have a sleeping bag or a blanket and warm clothes. You would be worried about losing them or being robbed.

▲ *Sheltering in a packing crate on the London streets. It is cold, damp and dirty but still better than nothing.*

You would have to ask people for food or eat the food that other people throw away. You would need to wash at street taps or in public toilets. Your skin, hair and clothes would soon be dirty. Even finding a toilet might be difficult.

▶ *Begging on the Bangkok streets, this young boy hopes people will give enough to get him through the day.*

It would be easy to get ill or injured but you would have no quiet, clean place to recover.

How would you get money? Finding a proper job would be hard, especially if you had no experience or were ill. Perhaps you could be a busker or clean car windows or sell papers. Chances are that you would probably find these jobs much harder than they look and you would face lots of competition. You might end up begging, or even stealing, to get enough money to survive.

Of course, some times might be better than others. During the summer, life might not be too difficult. But what happens when the skies pour rain, or sleet, or snow, when food is hard to come by and there are no places to shelter? How would you manage then?

'Being homeless can mean having no money, no security, no future.'
Shelter, housing charity, UK.

▼ *Night shelters for homeless people are often overcrowded. This man eats his food in the toilets.*

5

Universal problems

Homeless people come from many different backgrounds. There are children, women and men, young and old people. Each has a different story to tell about their life and different ideas about the world. In other words, they are individuals, just like you and me.

However, homeless people do share many experiences. Most come from families where money is tight and jobs are hard to come by. Many have experienced family problems or have been in children's homes or prison.

> 'Packing up and unpacking, packing up and unpacking. You'd just get comfortable and Dad would want to move again. So off we would go and start again.'
>
> *Homeless woman, USA.*

▲ *A homeless teenager on the streets. She has nowhere to go.*

case study · case study · case study · case study · case study

As a child, Martin never had a proper home. His family was always on the move. They rented houses, flats, even a mobile home. When they finally stopped moving, it was too late for Martin. He couldn't settle. He had never stayed anywhere long enough to make friends or keep up with schooling. His family wanted to help him but didn't know how. He began skipping school, and spending more and more time on the streets with other truants.

At first it was great. The group begged and busked on the streets and in the shopping malls. Sometimes they stole clothes or videos and CDs. It was only a matter of time before Martin was caught. He spent the following years in and out of court and ended up in prison.

When Martin left prison, he didn't want to see his family and his few friends had settled down. There were no jobs for a school drop-out with a criminal record. Martin became depressed and began drifting into a life on the streets.

▷ *Without money, family or friends, homeless people, like this young man, face a bleak future.*

A global issue

No one knows how many people are without a home. In countries where the government holds a regular census, homeless people are often uncounted. Many homeless people are not easy to contact because they move around. Others try to avoid government officials.

▲ *This family in Calcutta, India, lives and sleeps on the streets. They may stay here for years.*

Another problem is that numbers keep changing. Some people stay on the streets for a short time – maybe a night or two or a few weeks. Some return to their old homes. Others find shelter – maybe in a night shelter or hostel or sleeping on a friend's floor. The lucky ones find a proper home. But sometimes the days and weeks on the streets turn into months and years.

Some countries have many homeless people. The greatest numbers are found in poor developing countries where millions of people flock to the cities to seek work. Some find shelter, often sharing with friends and relatives, but others have nowhere to live.

Even when housing is available, it might cost too much or be too far away. Many people live on the streets, hoping that they will save enough for a home of their own.

In richer countries, fewer people live on the streets. Once again, most stay in the cities. Governments sometimes provide extra help with housing, especially for families and older people, but many homeless people are not able to get government help. Others don't want the government to interfere; they just want to be left alone to manage without help.

◀ *Some homeless people have spent years on the road.*

FACT:
Experts say that there are 100 million people world-wide without any shelter at all. This number includes people who sleep outside, in public buildings or in temporary night shelters.
Just imagine 100 million people – that's twice the population of England, or twenty times the population of countries such as Scotland or Denmark.
An Urbanizing World, UN Centre for Human Settlements, Geneva, Switzerland.

2. Why are people homeless?

How do people become homeless?

All over the world, millions of people are on the move. Some have been forced to move because their homes have been destroyed by natural disasters such as hurricanes, floods or earthquakes. Others have fled their homes in fear of their lives or have been driven out by invading armies. The lucky ones return and start to rebuild their lives and homes. However, many people never return home.

But most people move because they want a better life. One of the biggest movements is from the countryside to the cities. People seek work in the growing cities because it is harder to make a living from farming, herding and fishing. Others move to join family and friends who are already in the city or because they want fun and excitement – the 'buzz' of city life.

▲ *Slums built over an open sewer in Jakarta, capital of Indonesia.*

▶ *In Africa war has meant many children have lost their homes and families. These orphans have their names written on bandages on their head, so that aid workers can identify them.*

FACT:
In 1998 25 million people left their homes
because of the effects of natural disasters,
environmental problems and climate change.
In October 1998 Hurricane Mitch roared through
Central America. Fierce winds and driving rain
swept away entire landscapes including farms,
forests, roads, towns and villages. In a few days
3 million people lost their homes.

World Disasters Report,
International
Federation of the
Red Cross and
Red Crescent, 1999.

▲ *A little girl cuddles her dog amid the wreckage of her home, destroyed by Hurricane Mitch.*

One of the biggest problems for city-dwellers is housing. Often land is scarce and housing costs are high. Even when people find work, they may not be able to afford somewhere to live. Many stay in cheap boarding houses or shared rooms. Others live in the shanty towns that spring up on the outskirts, building their own homes from whatever materials they can find – wood, bricks, tin or plastic sheets.

In the worst cases people find themselves living on the streets, building small shelters on the pavements or sleeping rough in doorways and alleyways or under bridges or even in sewers under the city streets.

The true meaning of homelessness

What does it really mean to be without a home? Here are four types of homeless people:

♦ people without a roof – sleeping rough on the streets, in railway and bus stations or under bridges
♦ people without a house – sleeping in night shelters, hostels or other temporary shelters
♦ people in temporary houses – squatting in empty buildings, in shanty towns or refugee camps
♦ people in bad houses – lacking basic facilities, such as electricity or running water

For every one homeless person sleeping rough, there are many more who find some form of shelter.

▼ *This young man has a bed in a night shelter – but he is still homeless.*

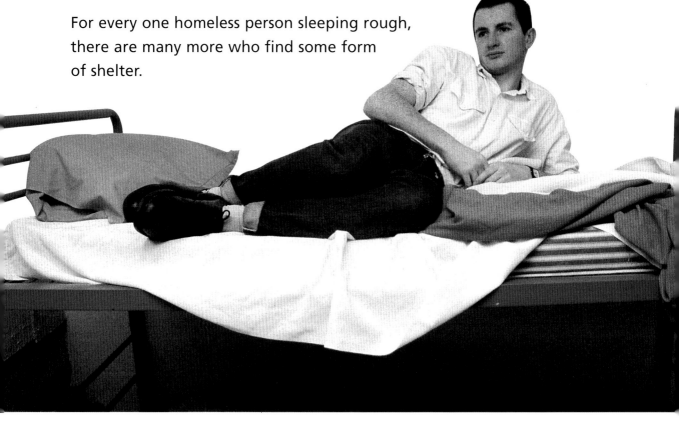

case study · case study · case study · case study · case study

Anita is ten years old and comes from Jaipur, one of the main cities in Rajasthan in India. She lives in a small hut. The walls are made from old bricks, the roof from tin and plastic sheets and the floor is the pavement. There is no running water or electricity. Anita's family use the hut to sleep, dress and store their few belongings, and cook, eat and work on the pavement outside.

Anita's parents left their village years ago. Now they make a living by ironing clothes for the better-off families who live nearby. Anita collects and delivers the heavy bundles of clothing, helps with washing and cooking and minds the younger children. Somehow she also manages to attend school, although she finds it hard to concentrate.

Despite all the problems, Anita's family prefers living in Jaipur to being in the village – at least they can make a living in the city and the children can attend school.

▲ *This little girl and her family live in a slum in Jaipur, India.*

"
'People come to the city looking for work and a livelihood. They are not looking for a home. They have homes in villages. They leave those homes to look for jobs. So even if their huts are knocked down in the city, they will sleep on pavements.'
Anand Patwardhan, film director, India.
"

Poverty and homelessness

People become homeless in many different ways. As we have seen, some people lose homes in natural disasters or in wars. But the most common reason for homelessness is poverty.

In simple terms, poverty means not having enough money to enjoy a good standard of life. There are many different ideas of what a good standard means. But, nearly everywhere, people agree that it should include:

♦ good quality food to stay healthy and active
♦ clean running water for drinking and washing
♦ basic goods such as clothes, shoes or furniture
♦ good, safe housing with room for everyone
♦ healthy neighbourhoods with facilities such as electricity, clean streets and regular rubbish collection

▼ *Washing up in the street. Squatters in Calcutta, India, must use public facilities such as this water tank.*

World-wide, millions of people are too poor to buy or rent a proper house or apartment. Some are unemployed but many work for wages. Even if the whole family works, they can't afford proper housing. Like Anita's family, many build their own homes wherever they can find a big enough space. Others occupy empty buildings.

▲ *Slums in the shadow of skyscrapers in Jakarta, Indonesia. Many families live in each small space.*

These people are known as 'squatters'. Most squatters don't have permission to be there, so they have no rights to either the land or the homes they have built. If they are lucky, they may be allowed to stay and go on to build a secure life.

▲ *Four children share one bed in a damp, cold room in a squat. Even in rich countries some families live in poor housing.*

But many squatters are forced out, or evicted. The land becomes more valuable, land prices rise and landlords decide to sell the land to richer people. City councils are often ashamed of squatter settlements; they say that squatters give the city a bad image. So squatters regularly face eviction. Their homes are knocked down, often without warning, and their belongings are destroyed. There is no compensation: people have to start all over again, trying to find somewhere else to live.

3. The search for shelter

Why aren't there enough houses for everyone?

As the patterns of people's lives change, so do their needs for housing. We have already seen how people in developing countries leave the countryside to seek jobs and a better life in the growing cities, despite the problems of finding somewhere to work and live.

Something similar happens in richer countries. Older industries find that the goods they make can be produced more cheaply elsewhere.

▶ *When people leave poor areas for more prosperous places, they become rundown and deserted. This area is in a poor part of Brooklyn, New York.*

FACT:
About 600 million city-dwellers in Africa, Asia and Latin America crowd into housing without running water or proper drainage and rubbish collection. As more people arrive, more homes will be needed.
An Urbanizing World,
UN Centre for Human Settlements, Geneva, Switzerland.

▶ *Rich and poor houses are often found side-by-side. This is Kingston, capital of Jamaica.*

As a result, factories close and jobs are lost. People look for new jobs and new houses in more prosperous areas. With fewer people to serve, shops, cafés, bars and cinemas make less money and many close down. Now there are even less jobs available, so more people move out. Only the oldest or poorest people stay on. Once friendly neighbourhoods become rundown or deserted.

On the other hand, houses may not be available in areas where people want to live. After all, who would choose to live in an area where there is heavy pollution or thundering traffic or a high crime rate? Most people prefer a safe friendly neighbourhood with clean air and good facilities such as schools and libraries. The result is that houses in the most popular areas are likely to rise in price. Some people can no longer afford to live there. They move to cheaper areas, where the housing and facilities are less good. Some become homeless.

FACT:
Each year about 25,000 people move from northern England to seek jobs in London and the south. As a result, some northern cities have rows of empty houses, while new houses are needed in southern England.
The Guardian, 1999.

No job, no home, no hope?

People move for many reasons – to seek work, to attend college, to get married or to be near other family members. Others want to leave their past behind and establish a new life in another area or another country. Most people do find new homes, even if they don't always find exactly what they are looking for. Finding a job is often the first step on the long road to finding a suitable home.

FACT:
A survey of homeless people in thirty American cities found that one in five had a job but couldn't afford a room.

Why are people homeless?
National Coalition for the Homeless, 1999.

▼ *High unemployment means that many people compete for available jobs.*

case study · case study · case study · case study · case study

Tom has been homeless since he left his family in the north of England six months ago. Not that it was much of a family – his father was never around and his mother found it hard to cope. So he was glad to leave.

But Tom couldn't find a job locally. So he hitched to London and stayed with friends. He found work with a fast food chain but couldn't find a room nearby that he could afford. He joined a group squatting in an empty house but the squatters were evicted after a few months. Tom returned to sleeping on people's floors but there were always problems – fights, drugs and noisy nights. He was so tired he was always late for work and got fired.

Tom wants to work and he wants somewhere to live. But it's difficult to find and keep a job without a proper place to live. And without a job, he can't afford somewhere to live. He feels trapped.

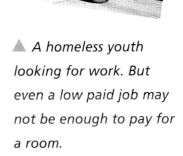

Unfortunately, not everyone finds a new home. As we have seen, millions of people live in extremely overcrowded buildings or sprawling shanty towns. But some people are forced to live on the streets or in temporary shelters because they cannot find a home:
♦ of the right size
♦ with the right facilities
♦ in the area they want to live
♦ at a price they can afford

▲ *A homeless youth looking for work. But even a low paid job may not be enough to pay for a room.*

The housing problem

Even when there is enough housing for everyone, some houses remain empty. The main reason is that houses are too expensive for people to afford to buy or rent. The most expensive housing is found in the richest cities, such as New York, Los Angeles, London, Paris, Sydney and Tokyo, especially in pleasant neighbourhoods with good quality buildings. Only the richest people can afford to live there.

But even outside these areas, houses are too expensive for many people. In many countries, governments limit the amount of land available for housing. This means land becomes even more scarce and more valuable. One result is that land is divided into smaller and smaller parcels, and houses and flats become smaller.

▲ *High-rise blocks in Hong Kong. In crowded cities where land is scarce, this is a common way to house people.*

'Poor people find it difficult to pay for housing, food, child care, health and education. Housing often takes the largest proportion of people's income. Being poor means being an illness, an accident or a paycheck away from living on the streets.'

National Coalition for the Homeless, USA.

Another problem is discrimination. Landlords who own or rent houses may prefer some types of people to others. For example, they may prefer single people to families, or local people to foreigners, or white people to black people – or maybe the other way round. People with disabilities, or families with small children, often find it very hard to get suitable housing.

Many countries now have laws saying that it is wrong to treat people differently because of their age, sex, colour, ethnic group or disability. However, despite these laws, discrimination sometimes continues. In any case, most people do not want to move to an area where they meet with prejudice and hostility. They prefer to live somewhere more friendly, even if this means they pay higher prices for housing.

▷ *Once this man had a job and a home. Now he has lost both and must beg on the streets of Washington DC, USA.*

4. Life on the streets

How do homeless people eat, sleep and work?

Life on the streets is a struggle; it's unpredictable and insecure. So, you might think that street people live a completely chaotic life. In fact, just like us, most homeless people try to develop a daily routine, doing certain things at certain times. This is not always possible, especially if you are forced to keep moving by police, officials and property owners. We met Anita and Martin earlier in the book. Here is a breakdown of their days:

▼ *An Indian girl spends a lot of her waking hours looking after younger brothers and sisters.*

Anita's day

05.15 – wakes up

05.30 – fetches milk

05.45 – sweeps pavement around hut

06.00 – fetches clothes for ironing from customers

07.00 – has bath and breakfast

07.30 – leaves for school

13.15 – returns from school, has leftovers for lunch

13.30 – delivers bundles of ironed clothes to customers

15.00 – sweeps and cleans, does homework

16.00 – fetches milk

16.30 – more deliveries to customers

21.00 – deliveries finally finish, dozes off exhausted

22.30 – woken to eat with parents

23.00 – sleeps, sharing rope bed with two younger sisters

Martin's day

05.00 – wakes up on pavement, as streets cleaners approach
05.15 – packs belongings, buys coffee from stall
06.00 – walks around, talks with other homeless people
07.30 – sits outside station begging from travellers, moved on by police
09.30 – buys breakfast, washes at public toilets
10.30 – walks across city in search of work, no luck
13.15 – begs from shoppers in mall, moved on by security guards
14.30 – finds half-eaten sandwich in bin, falls asleep in park
16.00 – attends drop-in clinic for treatment of old injury
17.30 – queues for hostel bed but hostel is full
19.30 – beds down on pavement
21.30 – wakes up, talks and drinks with other homeless people
24.00 – bread and soup delivered by charity
01.00 – drifts back to sleep on pavement

People in different circumstances have different routines. Anita, from India, who lives with her family on the pavement, and Martin, who sleeps rough in a big American city, both have to eat, sleep and wash. They have to do the everyday things that everybody, no matter who they are, do wherever they live.

▶ *This couple is used to eating and sleeping in doorways.*

Strength in numbers

Homeless people often band together to try to keep themselves safe and out of danger. They may share food, drink or drugs. They may watch out for each other or try to protect weaker people from being beaten up or moved on. Others are loners, preferring to rely on their own knowledge and skills to keep them safe on the streets.

Because they are smaller and weaker than adults, and are easier to bully and beat, homeless children are especially likely to band together.

▼ These children from Rio de Janeiro in Brazil are poor but have a home to go to. Other poor children live on the streets.

◀ Many homeless people spend their days in parks, bus stops and other public places. These two men stick together for companionship.

24

case study · case study · case study · case study · case study

Bekele lives on the streets of Addis Ababa, the capital of Ethiopia. He is eleven years old and has been homeless since his mother died two years ago. At first he was alone but now he belongs to a gang of other young boys who look out for each other.

The boys hang around the same area. They share the leftover food they get from hotels. They run errands, carry goods and look after parked cars. Sometimes they beg or steal. The older children try to protect the young ones and do their best to help those who are ill or injured. They fear being caught by shopkeepers or police, who often beat and imprison them.

Bekele is one of millions of homeless children around the world. Most live on the city streets of Asia, Africa and Latin America but there are also homeless children in richer countries. These children are often described as `street children'- although many do stay in touch with their family. Street children spend their days – and often their nights – on the streets.

▷ *Street children sleeping rough in Kigali, Rwanda. Many children lost their families in the war.*

Money matters

Homeless people find many ways to get money. In poorer countries, most homeless people work, often at the most difficult and dirty jobs. They may work on building sites, collect and recycle rubbish, or fetch and carry goods. But this work is insecure and poorly paid so it is very hard to earn and save enough to buy or rent a home.

▲ It's hard to find work if you are alone with a baby to care for too. This young Russian mother has to beg for money.

Work is not only for adults. In many countries, children also earn money, often by providing some sort of service – running errands, carrying shopping, shining shoes, serving in small hotels or tea shops, sorting rubbish. Some search the streets for bottles or cardboard that can be resold for a tiny profit. Some children beg or steal, either individually or as part of a group or gang.

▼ Women in South Africa earn money making bricks.

In richer countries, it is much harder to find this sort of work. For example, people shop at supermarkets, goods are carried by van, and rubbish collection and recycling is done by machines. Many regular jobs require a good education or special skills. Many homeless people do not have the education or skills to get a job.

If they are ill, or have addictions or personal problems, they may not be able to work regularly. And as we have seen, without a proper address, it is more difficult to find a job.

As a result, many homeless people either beg from passers-by or depend on charity. A few earn money by busking – playing music, singing or dancing. Some find odd jobs or get rewarded for small services. Some sell newspapers or deliver leaflets. In some countries, homeless people get social security from government or small payments, food or medical care from charities. Most barely manage.

▲ *Busking on the streets is one way to earn money. This boy plays for onlookers in Krakow, Poland.*

'They just don't want to work.'
Passer-by, Sydney, Australia.

'I'd like to work, but who will employ someone like me?'
Homeless person, New York, USA.

27

5. Health and safety

Is street life dangerous?

Will you live to a ripe old age? The chances are that you will still be alive when you are seventy, even eighty, and so will most of your friends. But a person living on the streets is not so lucky. Their health is so badly affected by living rough that most die by the time they are forty-five or fifty.

Street life ages people quickly. They are outside in all weathers. They eat bad food and they are more likely to catch diseases. It's hard to keep clean without running water and regular shelter. The streets can also be violent, especially after dark. Sleeping outside means they make easy targets for vicious attacks from other people. Many street people are probably much younger than you think.

'I'd rather die on the streets than in hospital.'
Homeless man,
Paris, France.

'Would you want to sit in a doctor's waiting room next to a dirty street person?'
Nurse working with homeless men,
Glasgow, Scotland.

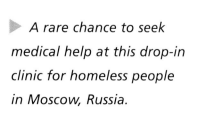

A rare chance to seek medical help at this drop-in clinic for homeless people in Moscow, Russia.

case study · case study · case study · case study · case study

Mike has lived on the streets for years. He is in his thirties but looks much older. Although he is tough, he is actually very sick. He coughs a lot and his skin is covered with sores.

Mike is sick because he eats left-over food from garbage cans. He catches diseases when he sleeps in crowded shelters. Although Mike tries to keep clean and dry, it's hard without running water and proper shelter.

Mike knows that he is ill but he doesn't want to go to the hospital. He doesn't trust doctors or nurses. In any case, he has no money to pay for medicines or a quiet place to recover.

Homeless people find it difficult to get medical treatment. They often have special problems, like lung diseases or sore, rotten feet. They may be frightened or ashamed to see a doctor or to go to a hospital. In some cases they are too poor to pay for medical help.

▲ *Alone in the snow, a homeless man tries to sleep on a bench in an American city park.*

Drink, drugs and homelessness

Some homeless people are addicted to a substance, and drink alcohol, sniff glue, inject heroin or become involved in an activity like gambling. An addict is a person who has a desperate need that can only be satisfied by having more of the substance or activity. People can be cured of different addictions but treatment is nearly always long and expensive.

Sometimes, addictions lead to homelessness. A person may spend everything on their addiction, and fall behind with their rent or mortgage payments. Others leave home after family arguments, especially if they have been stealing to pay for their addiction. After they become homeless, they can still remain addicts.

▼ Some homeless people are addicted to alcohol or hard drugs. Without help, it is difficult to overcome their addiction. These Russian men drink vodka from an old water bottle.

A homeless teenager watches passers-by in London. Alone on the streets, he faces many dangers.

"

'I don't blame people for walking past. I suppose they think I'm already dead.'
Homeless man, London.

"

Addiction, a poor diet and bad living conditions affect their health. The only way to survive might be to sell drugs or their own body for sex. In some countries, addiction is responsible for half the crimes recorded by police.

On the other hand, people may become addicted after they become homeless. Drinking alcohol or taking drugs may help them to cope with day-to-day life on the streets. A cold night or an empty stomach might be warmed by alcohol or sniffing glue. And, if the people around you drink or take drugs, it's easy to fall into the same habits.

FACT:
Most homeless people are not addicts. Some may drink alcohol or take drugs but they do not become addicts. Alcohol or drugs are only a small part of their problems. However, many homeless people are in bad health or have mental illness.
Shelter, Housing Charity, UK, 1997.

Street-life dangers

Life on the streets can be extremely dangerous and unpredictable. Remember, even people with a home worry about being robbed or attacked. Imagine how much more frightening life would be if you had no home to go to, no family to protect you.

Here are a few of the things that make street life difficult and dangerous:

♦ going hungry and eating poor quality food

♦ drinking too much alcohol

♦ sharing dirty needles

♦ being pushed into dangerous or criminal activities

♦ being robbed or losing your few possessions

♦ being arrested or moved on by police or officials

♦ being attacked and beaten by street people, by gangs, by police or passers-by

♦ being run down by cars, mostly by accident but sometimes deliberately

♦ being evicted, sometimes violently, from temporary homes such as squats, pavement dwellings or shanty towns

FACT:
Homeless people in London are 150 times more likely to be murdered than other people.
Shelter, Housing Charity, UK, 1992.

▶ *A family in the Philippines eat by the roadside. Although they are without shelter and find themselves eating in unclean places, they have each other for support.*

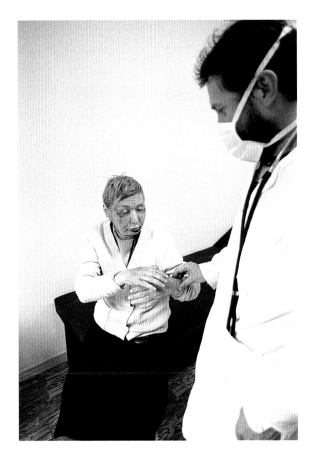

'People tell me to get off the streets and go to a night shelter. Night shelters are dirty and dangerous. You are more likely to get robbed in a shelter than on the street. Often they won't let you take your dog in either. I prefer to take my chances outside.'

Homeless man, New York.

◀ *Beaten and bruised, this woman has fled a violent home. But can she find a safe haven?*

The smallest and weakest people face the greatest risks. In some countries, gangs and police have deliberately attacked and killed children living on the streets. Young teenagers, girls and boys, have been picked up by criminals who force them to sell their bodies or push them into crime.

▲ *A homeless woman in the Philippines. All her belongings are on the pavement after she has been turned out of her squatter home.*

Homeless women, and their children, have special problems. Many women have stayed in violent homes for many years, hoping that things would improve. They didn't want to leave but were forced out by violence. Many find themselves without support, and have to live on the streets, in hostels, shelters or squats.

6. Supporting street people

How can we help people to leave the streets?

Most homeless people don't want to be on the streets. Just like other people, they want a proper home. However, they face huge difficulties:

♦ finding a place to live at a price they can afford
♦ getting enough money to pay rent and bills
♦ tackling personal problems, like illness or addictions
♦ overcoming prejudice against street people
♦ learning new tasks, like cooking, cleaning and paying bills
♦ getting used to a settled way of life, instead of being on the move

Many homeless people are frightened and feel that they couldn't cope with the responsibility of looking after a home. They may have fled from a violent home, only to face further violence on the streets. They may feel worthless – good for nothing. Their biggest difficulty is to learn to believe in themselves, to feel that they can cope with a settled life away from the life they know on the streets.

Support from the staff at a drop-in centre can be the first step towards a life away from the streets.

Groups who work with homeless people know that leaving the streets can take time. A gradual step-by-step approach is often the only way.

The first step is to gain people's trust. This might be followed by practical help, such as a drop-in centre where people can store their possessions or talk with a doctor or nurse. The next step might be to persuade rough sleepers to use night shelters or hostels, especially in cold or wet weather. In turn, this encourages people to look to the future and to start thinking about finding permanent housing.

Not everyone wants to leave the streets. Some people have been on the move for so long they can't even begin to imagine settling down. Others find street life interesting and exciting. Some homeless people prefer life on the streets to living in a violent or unhappy home.

▲ A street kitchen to feed homeless people, run by a charity. Some people prefer living on the streets but help is still welcome.

▶ Some people are so used to a life outside that they don't want to settle down.

Providing extra support

Finding a home is not the end of the story. Homeless people often need extra support to help them stay off the streets. For example, the local council or a charity might supply low rent housing and help with heating or bedding and furniture. Who wants to move into a cold empty room? Settling down can be very strange, particularly if it is in an unfamiliar neighbourhood.

> 'Giving people a place to live is only the start. They need extra help. One man panicked every time he got a bill. We had to explain them and show him how to pay. Other people had to learn how to shop or cook.'
>
> *Worker supporting homeless people, Sheffield, UK.*

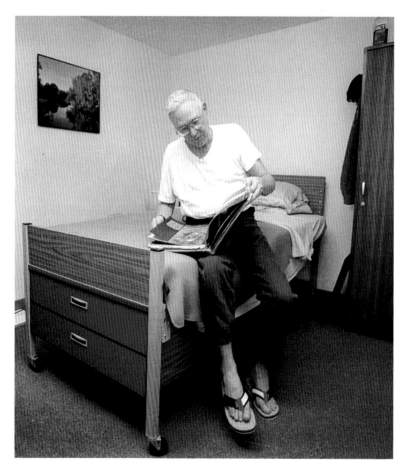

◀ *Once this man was a soldier in Vietnam. Then he spent years on the streets. Now, at last, he can relax in a room provided for him by a special charity.*

case study · case study · case study · case study · case study

Marie was overjoyed when she finally got her own flat. Ever since she had left home years before, she had wanted somewhere to call her own. She had been in and out of children's homes, temporary hostels and bed-and-breakfast hotels. Now she had her own flat and her own tiny baby.

But life was much more difficult than she imagined. Her new flat had hardly any furniture, the carpet was threadbare and it was often cold. Her social security payments had to cover rent, heating and electricity as well as food and clothes. She wasn't used to cooking meals or paying bills and the baby wouldn't stop crying.

But the worst thing was the loneliness. The flat was a long way from the city centre. She felt cooped up all day, every day. She went to the shops and the health centre but she knew no-one. She had left her former friends behind. When she was homeless she had often been cold and frightened but she had never been so lonely.

▶ *A young single mother cuddles her baby. Everyone wants a safe and secure place to give their children a good start in life.*

Getting ready to work

As we have seen, most homeless people find it hard to get work. Many have dropped out of school and lack job skills. Even turning up to work on time can be a struggle. When work is available, it is likely to be badly paid and insecure.

There are special schemes to help street people find work. Sometimes homeless people get together to help themselves. Today, in many towns and cities it is common to see homeless people selling street papers. They buy papers at a lower price and sell them for a higher price. The profit provides a small income – the first step to a life off the streets.

▼ *A hand-up, not a hand-out. Selling the* Big Issue *on the city streets.*

'A group of us wanted to help homeless people find work.
If you are homeless and need a job, you need a place to get clean, have clean clothes and have a place to store your belongings. So we called our group SHWASHLOCK – SHowers, WASHers and LOCKers.'

Homeless woman, California.

▲ *A street child in Cape Verde, west Africa, at a training session. With a skill he can earn money and leave the streets.*

Street papers aim to give 'a hand-up, not a hand-out'. Gaining confidence is just as important as earning money. Homeless people discover new skills, such as handling money, learning sales patter, mixing with other people. Street papers also show the general public, people like you and me, that homeless people are able to help themselves.

In many countries there are special schemes to help street children. Drop-in centres and safe houses give children opportunities to catch up on lost schooling as well as to learn skills to earn money to support themselves. As a result, children have a better chance to escape the dangerous streets and the criminal gangs that prey on them.

FACT:
Street News, the world's first street paper, started in New York city in 1989.
A year later *the Big Issue* appeared in London. Now there are almost 100 street papers world-wide.

The Big Issue,
London, UK.

7. Looking for solutions

What can we do to end homelessness?

Homelessness is not a new problem. When we look at the past, we can find many periods when homelessness was common. For example, in sixteenth century England, it was recorded that one in four people were 'roaming vagabonds' – homeless people without land and homes. Coming forward to 1930s America, millions of poor farmers lost their farms to drought and dust-storms. As we have seen, today millions of people in developing countries live as homeless pavement dwellers or squatters.

▲ A street child in nineteenth century Britain. In big cities, groups of poor children lived and worked on the streets.

As countries become richer, we would expect the numbers of homeless people to start to fall. But this is not always the case. In fact, it appears that in some countries the numbers have risen. Although most people are doing well, conditions become harder for the poorest people.

> 'Only five per cent of people sleeping rough do so from choice. The most common reason is the breakdown of relations with parents or a partner. Between one quarter and one third of rough sleepers have been in children's homes or foster care.'
>
> *Report of the Social Exclusion Unit, UK Government, 1999.*

Studies of homeless people in rich countries, such as in Europe, the USA and Australia, paint a depressing picture. They reveal that:

♦ most homeless people come from poor families

♦ many homeless people have dropped out of school or lack job skills

♦ many young homeless people have been in children's homes or in foster care or have run away from home

♦ many homeless people have been in juvenile detention or in prison

♦ many homeless women and children lose their homes after families split up

♦ some people become homeless because they are mentally ill or have addictions

♦ many homeless people get some government support but others miss out

♦ many homeless people could find a home if cheaper housing was available

▲ Many homeless people have spent time in juvenile detention or in prison.

▼ Sheltering in a night café, a homeless man has a cup of tea and a quiet nap.

Stopping people from becoming homeless

As we have seen, there are many ways in which governments and charities try to help people living on the streets – providing money and food, medical care and legal advice. These efforts are very important and they do help many people. But they don't tackle the underlying reasons why people become homeless.

Homelessness is a bit like a revolving door – as soon as one person goes out another comes in. We need to find ways to stop people coming through the door – to prevent them from becoming homeless in the first place.

Most people, even the poorest, usually cope on a day-to-day basis. But coping in a crisis, when everything seems to happen at once, can be much more difficult. At the worst times, when people are in greatest need of help, the support they need isn't available.

▼ *Volunteers at a drop-in centre for homeless people, help to cook and serve food to young people.*

Think of some of the ways that we could reach out to help people in these situations. Sometimes the answer might be more money, for example, to help people pay rent or a mortgage or to start special housing schemes for homeless people. But it might be other things, such as education, job training, treatment for addictions, support for broken families and cheaper housing. Often the needs are so big that only government action can make a difference.

▲ Nowhere else to go. A homeless man protests against a city law that bans homeless people from sleeping on city pavements in Detroit, USA.

'We managed okay with mortgage payments. Then I lost my job. We couldn't afford the mortgage anymore and ended up losing our house.'
Homeless man, Manchester, UK.

'After my wife died, I just couldn't cope. I cut myself off from everyone and started drinking. I ended up on the streets.'
Homeless man, New York, USA.

'After my mum remarried I just couldn't get on with my new stepdad. I ran away from home and started sleeping on people's floors.'
Homeless teenager, Sydney, Australia.

'First I was in care and then I was in prison. Who's going to employ an ex-prisoner, especially one without a place to live?'
Homeless teenager, Birmingham, UK.

Homes – great and small

When we look at people's homes, we realize that they come in many different types and sizes. Some are large and many are very small. Some families have two homes. Others have to share one or two rooms in run-down buildings. Some people live in temporary shelters or hostels or sleep on the streets.

Do we end homelessness by building more homes or sharing what we have more fairly? Do we help people after they become homeless, or do we try to stop them becoming homeless in the first place by giving them the help they need when life becomes difficult? What do you think?

▲ *A Chinese father and son stand proudly outside their flat. Their flat may be small but it is clean and well-maintained.*

◄ *A brand new home for this family in Malaysia. There is plenty of room and space to play.*

case study · case study · case study ·

More than anything, Nina wants her own bedroom. She hates sharing with her sisters. Her older sister guards her space fiercely and warns Nina not to touch her things. Her little sister makes such a mess that Nina is always tidying up after her.

Some of Nina's friends have their own rooms. One even has a separate playroom. `Lucky thing,' thinks Nina. `My own room, decorated the way I want – that would be bliss.'

But Nina knows that things could be much worse. Some of her school friends share rooms with three or more people. Their families can't afford a bigger place.

▲ *Sharing a room, even when you get on well together, can sometimes be a strain.*

She also knows two girls who live in hotels. Nina thought it sounded great until she discovered that these were special hotels for homeless families. Each family lives and sleeps in one room and has to wait in line to use one kitchen. There is no room to play and the girls can't invite friends to drop in. Nina's mum says that in some countries tiny children live on the streets, without proper homes or families. She says Nina should be grateful she only shares with her sisters.

GLOSSARY

Addiction
When a person has a desperate need for something, such as alcohol or drugs, and cannot give it up without help.

Bed-and-breakfast
Temporary housing – often residents have to leave each morning and spend their days on the streets.

Busking
Entertainment performed in the street.

Census
When the government tries to count every person living in a country.

Charity
A group that aims to help people or provide something without making a profit.

Compensation
A payment to make up for loss or damage.

Discrimination
Treating people differently and unfairly, often because of their colour or sex.

Drop-in centre
Services people can use without an appointment.

Environmental problems
Poisoning of land, water and air, or land erosion.

Eviction
An order by a landlord or council to leave an area or building/home.

Hostel
Temporary accommodation, normally sharing rooms with other people.

Landlord
Property owner. Can be a person, a company, a charity or a government agency.

Mental illness
Sickness of the mind, sometimes caused by stress, alcohol or drugs.

Mortgage
Loan to buy a property, usually paid off over a long period of time.

Night shelter
Temporary bed and facilities for homeless people (often run by charities).

Recycle
Collect and convert waste for new uses.

Refugee
Person who flees their country to escape persecution.

Rent
Payments to a landlord for use of a property.

Rough sleeper
Person who sleeps in the open – usually in the street.

Safe house
A safe and secure place, free from outside dangers.

Sales patter
Persuading people to buy your goods.

Social security
Payments by the government, usually to people who are ill, disabled, unemployed or caring for family members.

Squat
Occupying an empty or unused building or land without the permission of the owner.

Squatter settlements
Makeshift homes constructed on empty, unused or waste land, often against the law.

ORGANIZATIONS

World-wide, there are many organizations working to end homelessness. The organizations below can supply further information

Australia
The Council to Homeless Persons
Level 5, 140 Queen Street
Melbourne, Victoria 3000
Australia
www.infoxchange.net.au/
homeless/

Canada
National Anti-Poverty
Organization
256 King Edward Ave, Suite 316
Ottawa, Ontario K1M 7MI
Canada

Ireland
Focus Ireland
14a Eustace Street
Dublin 2
www.focusireland.ie/homeless

UK
Homeless International
Guildford House
20 Queens Road
Coventry CV1 3EG

Shelter
88 Old Street
London EC1V 9HU
www.shelter.org.uk

Shelter Cymru
25 Walter Road
Swansea SA1 1ZZ

Shelter (Northern Ireland)
165 University Street
Belfast BT17 1HR

Shelter (Scotland)
8 Hamilton Terrace
Edinburgh EH12 5JD

Y Care International
4th floor
3–9 Southampton Row
London WC1B 5HA
e-mail:
enq@ycare.ymca.org.uk

USA
National Coalition for the
Homeless
1012 Fourteenth Street NW
#600
Washington DC 20005-3410
e-mail: nch@ari.net
http://nch.ari.net/

FURTHER READING

Books for children
'Communities' School Resources Pack
(Homeless International and Bradford Education, 1999)
Doorways
by Barbara Taylor
(Save the Children, 1992)
Homes for all?
(Council for Education in World Citizenship, 1997)
Human Rights
by Kate Haycock
(Hodder Wayland, 1993)
Taking Action: Shelter
(Heinemann, 1997)
Talking Points: Homelessness
by Kaye Stearman
(Hodder Wayland, 1998)
When is a house not a home?
(Shelter)

Fiction
Hiding out
by Elizabeth Laird
(Mammouth, 1994)
Street Child
by Berlie Doherty
(Hamish Hamilton/Collins, 1993)
The Bed and Breakfast Star
by Jacqueline Wilson
(Corgi Yearling, 1995)

Further reading
Your local street paper

INDEX